Salt Lick Prayer

poems by

Lesley Brower

Finishing Line Press
Georgetown, Kentucky

Salt Lick Prayer

Copyright © 2017 by Lesley Brower
ISBN 978-1-63534-080-8 First Edition
All rights reserved under International and Pan-American Copyright Conventions. No part of this book may be reproduced in any manner whatsoever without written permission from the publisher, except in the case of brief quotations embodied in critical articles and reviews.

ACKNOWLEDGMENTS

My thanks to the editors of the journals in which some of these poems originally appeared, some in different forms, and many under my maiden name of Doyle.

Adanna, "Passalong Plants"
ALBATROSS, "Driving Through My Hometown in the Rain"
The Aurorean, "My Great, Great Grandfather Dreams of Returning Home" and "Heading South"
Big Muddy, "Flood Warning"
Blue Collar Review, "Drought"
The Dead Mule School of Southern Literature, "Riverside Elegy"
Deep South Magazine, "The Morning after the Haying"
Flutter, "Magic Lilies"
Hobble Creek Review, "False Spring"
Kudzu Review, "Salt Lick Prayer"
Pegasus, "Homestead"
Southern Women's Review, "The Offering"

Publisher: Leah Maines

Editor: Christen Kincaid

Cover Art: Holly Mathis Design

Author Photo: Bryan Brower

Cover Design: Holly Mathis

Printed in the USA on acid-free paper.
Order online: www.finishinglinepress.com
 also available on amazon.com

Author inquiries and mail orders:
Finishing Line Press
P. O. Box 1626
Georgetown, Kentucky 40324
U. S. A.

Table of Contents

Some Small Thievery 1
Crows 2
Sundown Devils 3
The Trouble with Tire Swings 4
Turkey Vulture 5
Controlled Burn 6
Summer Solstice 7
The Offering 8
Forecast 9
The Morning after the Haying 10
Fire-Talker 11
Pedestrian 12
Cow Tippin', 1998 13
Baptism 14
False Spring 15
Aubade for a Hummingbird 16
Magic Lilies 17
Love Poem 18
The First Draft of This Poem Had a Luna Moth in It ... 19
Late Migration 20
Pumpkin Vines 21
The Weaning 22
Flood Warning 24
When It Comes Down to It 25
Horse Thief 26
Laura May 29
The Basket Trees 31
Solomon Cradles His Firstborn 32

The Listing 33
My Great, Great Grandfather Dreams of
    Returning Home 35
Crossing out of Kentucky in a Cessna 172 36
Heading South 37
Driving Through My Hometown in the Rain 38
Homestead 39
My Great Grandmother Speaks of Wildfire 42
The Last Story My Great Grandmother Ever Told 43
Passalong Plants 44
Tornado Watch 45
Letters from the Arboretum 46
Drought 48
Buck Scouting, 1944 50
Riverside Elegy 51
Riverside Elegy II 52
Coyote 53
Salt Lick Prayer 54

In memory of Loy Edwin Houchin, my Pa

Some Small Thievery

June. Wet heat. No movement
save for the quivering net of gnats
rising from low clumps of jewelweed and sedge,
the mud-dull back of a snapping turtle
easing through clay at the river's edge.

All day I have been waiting
for some small thievery—
for the kestrel's swift raid
on a vole burrow, for the moist palm
of wind to flatten a cattail stand,
for the algae-flecked river
to carry past something
other than the flotsam
of overhanging trees.

Forgive me if today
I cannot appreciate the stillness.
We are on the cusp of summer.
My green heart has not yet gone to seed.

Crows
> *Richardsville, Kentucky*

Sure, I've watched a murder of them
claim a power line, sidestep
along the sagging cable, turning
the horizon into a hustle
of slate wing and hooked toes.

And plenty have made that last-second
flight in front of my car, rising
from the harvest of a broken corpse
at the roadsides crumbled edge.

But once, headed for the banks
of some nameless tributary,
I heard their graveled bray, topped a hill,

and saw—I swear it is true—thousands
of crows cloaking a valley of farmland
and the oak-spiked hills around it.

I don't remember what I caught that day,
if my bait snagged
the mouth of bluegill or crappie,
whether the water was clear or muddied
with rain-churn—I only remember the crows,

how they rose in a sooty tide
over the stubble of soybeans,
how they shrouded every tree,
how the sky, for an instant,
became a single, feathered heartbeat.

Sundown Devils

Truck backed far enough down
the gravel and grit boat ramp
that with the tailgate lowered
we can almost kick the river,
edges gone sluggish
with mud and algae, bits
that look just plain tired,
like the rest of us.

We bunch burlap behind our necks
and stretch out in the truck bed,
flex fingers sore from spiking burley,
suck splinters from our palms.

Sunset comes down thick,
wavy as molasses in the heat.
A coyote squalls off to one side.
No answer, just the river
slow and quiet and the *tic-tic*
of the engine still cooling.

When the mosquitoes start in on us,
we slap at our ankles, scratch the quick welts
until they bleed. We swat,
they sway and dart back in,
little sundown devils with mercy enough
to consume us all, give us wings.

The Trouble with Tire Swings

I still think of it, that rope and rubber pendulum
I threaded with the soft ribbon
of my body, the field-worn tread a stein
cupping rancid rainwater or the thin scaffolding
of cobwebs in its gummy dark.
Some nights, my body summons
the shiver of the rope-gartered branch,
the tense-and-shove takeoff of bare feet
against worn earth, and I wake as though pitched,
inches away from pressing through
the shadow-flecked canopy of leaves
and into the paling sky beyond,
the clouds floating belly-up, white,
like the flicked tails of fleeing deer.

Turkey Vulture

For hours I have been shucking Silver Queen
on the back porch, tugging husks
from tip to hilt and unweaving the mess

of silk from each ear, filling grocery bags
with stripped corn while the sheddings
scuttle about the deck. And for hours

I have been watching the same vulture
tilt and arc above the now-empty field.

(There could be carrion among
the splintered stalks, the body of a rabbit
or squirrel left in the combine's wake.)

Gleaner of the dead. Haunter of battlefields.
Is there a bird less loved? Ugly, voiceless,
they hiss or grunt or vomit when threatened,
they consume without pretense, without ceremony.

There is something in their faces, though,
that I have almost come to appreciate,
a creased wisdom in the purpled skin

around the eyes. I, too, have imagined
the taste of death on the back of my tongue,
felt the bitter gall of it go to seed in my gut.

I fear that if I don't busy my hands,
soon I'll sprout black remiges of my own,
take to the skies, join that dark bird,
and lose myself forever
in an endless dihedral drift.

Controlled Burn

We stripped splinters from the slatted fence
while eight acres blazed, the rattlesnake hiss and twitch
of flames waving like wheat, birthing heat into the sky.

I could talk now of nutrient exposure, debris removal,
but in truth, it was dry season then and reckless to begin with,
a sparking plea for life that scratched the ground black.

I know what it is to have been born of fire,
to let love sting my eyes like smoke, and to feel,
beneath the palm-curve of my ribs, the match-gutter
of my heart, an open field veined with flame.

Summer Solstice

Desperate for something to praise,
I have waited all day for God
to flash His bright teeth like light
sparking on a chipped lure
just above the minnowed surface of a pond—

but all in all nothing has changed,
just the same small tragedy of sunset,
the same stars coughing up broken beams
from between the pine boughs,
the same moths launching themselves
at the moon's shadowed crust.

The pears have begun to loosen their hold
on the trees. Fireflies cap and uncap
little lamps over the saccharine rot.
I too have grown ripe in my skin.
What stem holds me fast to this earth?

The Offering
> *For my father*

No tame thing grew that spring.

Maple seedlings sprouted from the gutter,
ivy pythoned the mailbox, and the yard,
rain-drunk, was a knee-deep tousle
of ragweed and stray bermudagrass.

With that first mowing,
dandelion spores parachuted
with each step you took.
We hadn't talked in days,
but I watched from the porch stoop,
made lazy from heat and the grunted lullaby
of a toad in the drainpipe.

That evening, you knelt in front of me,
smelling of gasoline and fescue and fatigue,
and uncupped your sunspotted hands
to reveal a nestling rabbit who had leapt
from the lawnmowers grated thrum.

That look on your face,
I still don't know what it meant.
But when you passed that tiny cottontail
to me, I could swear it was love itself
you were offering, a dark-eyed, shivering thing
that only wanted to be let loose.

Forecast

My mother says I was born on a day like this,
when the sun guttered behind grey clouds
and rotting oak leaves clogged the storm drain,
weeks after the cicadas stopped singing.

On the porch today, she points to the charcoal spine
of a caterpillar, tells me we're in for a rough winter.

Across the pasture, it begins to rain.
Cattle rise to their knees,
bowed heads nearly touching the ground,
that in itself a kind of prayer.

The Morning after the Haying

Raw-armed after a day of hoisting bales
from the shorn field to the flatbed
trailer, having paced in the diesel-thick wake
of tractor exhaust, dust, grasshoppers
lifting in waves from timothy and alfalfa,

I rise and find that Japanese beetles
have made lace of my tomato vines,
broad leaves thinned overnight,
spilling a patchwork of light
through chewed holes and frayed stems.

I don't know why I am in love with this land.
Kudzu cables shut the shed door
while speargrass and ironweed
choke out the half-runners.

Even the sandhill cranes won't stay,
only skim through near year's end.
Their ashed pinions ink the horizon.

And yes, I am tired too of evangelism,
single pump gas stations, Skoal rings,
of hominy, of crappie, of the seven different ways
to pronounce *Louisville*—

—so what is it that I feel when a peppered surge
of starlings swarm the neighboring field,
rising and holding for a moment
as the humid thrust of sunrise breaks the horizon
with its hot fingertip of devotion?

Fire-Talker
    For Clifford and Naomi Ray

Years ago, sedated with the chore-numb flow
of blanching the season's last bushel of Silver Queen—

tonging the husked ears into a roiling salt-bath
before cooling and coaxing kernels from the pocked cob—

my hand lingered too long above the kettles un-lidded mouth
and a lariat of steam seared the prophet-lines
of my palm, the thinly webbed forks between each finger.

I called a fire-talker, a luthier from a few farms over,
who showed up in my kitchen with sawdust-dredged boots,
flaxen curls of wood barnacling his jeans.

No small talk. He placed his lips above my blistering palm
and began to whisper. I couldn't hear his words,
but I felt the breath-weight of their pressure.
You've already decided whether or not you believe
this story, and that's fine. All I know is that by nightfall

the welts receded, the pain ebbed back into the pulse-tide
of my body, and my raw fingers forked bite after bite
of creamed corn into my stupid, thankful mouth.

Pedestrian

In the year before my birth,
scientists spliced the genes of a firefly
with those of a tobacco strain,
planted acres of five-foot burley—
glowing fronds, the belly-gleam
of those twilight torches fused, sewn,
risen again from anchoring soil.

I was raised in more pedestrian rows,
coarse-leaved labyrinths birthed
from the chapped ground,
thick walls of green-going-to-yellow,
milk thistle and morning glory vines
jungleing clean furrows each night.

I have planted in those fields,
plucked hornworms thick as thumbs
from leaves, measured the height
of crowns with my palm
until I could reach no higher.
I have watched them stand
through the bitter crisp of drought,
slump through the mold and wilt
of flood, and now and again I have paused,
listened to the wasp-winged rustle
of their quiet rearranging at dusk,
and that, too, is luminous.

Cow Tippin', 1998

For the record, I wasn't the one
who pushed the cow. I was the one

who held the flashlight, its dim beam
clarifying and dismissing the tips

of tobacco sticks, rusted combine blades,
the brailed backs of feed sacks.

I was the one at the edge of the pasture,
pressed against the fence, feeling guilty

at the sound of startled lowing,
the heavy-lidded eyes rising, shoved from sleep.

Baptism

The creek defied season, remaining an icy runnel
even in the height of summer. When I took that first step,
arms outstretched to the pastor already waist-deep in the water,

I forgot the congregation lining the half-moon bank,
hymns of blessing lifting from each mouth,
singing of the water, of the river, of that bright by-and-by.

I trembled, balanced on lichen-slick stone,
minnows billowing around my ankles in a quaking cloud,
my skin gone gooseflesh from cold and nerves.

The pastor steadied me, river foaming at our hips *I baptize this, my sister,*
my hand lifted in his *in the name of the Father*
dress current-bound to my body *in the name of the Son,*

tree branches sifting shadow and sunlight *and of the Holy Spirit.*
A drawn breath, my hand over my mouth,
the pastor's practiced release of me into the stream.

My ears filled with quiet wasp-in-a-bottle-buzz, easy womb-pulse,
then the water shattered and resealed as I broke from it,
gasping, everything once again bright and loud.

If there is a true stillness, it must be that heavy climb
to the bank, river-water clumping my lashes,
towels girding my shoulders, wicking the drip of my hair.

It must be the lapping chill of that river
and the non-silence beneath its brim
in which I could have lain, weightless, forever.

False Spring

Daybreak shreds the glinted rind
of winter's latest frost, each blade

of fescue cocooned in a bright,
dripping shroud, tree limbs flexing,

rinsing themselves in light, paring
away the iced remains of a season

pretending to pass. Dead leaves bird-hop
in quick circles. Sparrows preen

in bare branches, peck at the unsewn
patchwork of my flowerbeds.

I know this false spring will soon end,
give way to more days of snow puckered

at the base of each tree like laundry
blown from the line, crystalline sheets

knotted beneath the row of elms,
slumped against the fencerow's edge.

But today I cannot loose myself
from the bright riot of it all,

this world ablaze
with sunlight and birdsong.

Today, I still have enough audacity to pray.
Today, I believe it is heard.

Aubade for a Hummingbird

Bright whirr by my ear,
more color than sound,

        the emerald blur of a hummingbird
        in whip-stitch flight, flickering

by the eves then blinking
near the hollyhocks,

        quick hover and dart
        into each warm bloom.

Even after its passing,
the whole garden still aquiver

        with wingbeat,
        that shuddering space

between what is taken
and what is left behind.

Magic Lilies
    Lycoris squamigera

—as if milky rabbits could be drawn from their throats,
silken scarves slipped from a sleeve of soil, audiences captivated
as each petal unfolds, damply etched with prophecy—

but no, here is what happens: bare ground, and then overnight
giraffe-legged stalks flex skyward, sprout fluted blossoms—
a trick so tangible you could almost press your ear to the ground
and hear the marble-roll growl of something ancient giving birth.

Love Poem

My bones thrum
to the tune bees sing
into the open mouths
of apple blossoms. I, too,
am restless for touch.
You fluster my grip
on this earth, set me skyward
in a sun-flushed whirl.
How easily I am unhinged,
lifted, set aflame.

The First Draft of This Poem Had a Luna Moth in It

and even though I've taken it out, my lines are dusted in moss-green;
they fray at the edges the more I touch them.

My entire second stanza has become nocturnal,
and shivers away from the bright tip of my pen.

Even my metaphors have grown antennae
and are trying to lay eggs on the bellies of black walnut leaves.

Late Migration

Midnight and quiet, frost
just beginning to spider
the grass, trees lost
in the somnolent sway and creak
of trunk against trunk,
and then a shiver, a frayed sash
in the sky, a flitting
absence and return of stars
and the call of geese,
a clamored burst twining
past the scant canopy, straining
through the darkness and cold,
hymn of journey swept down,
the soft percussion of branches keeping time.

Pumpkin Vines

Still fumbling with the latch
of consciousness, I wake
thinking of the pumpkin plants
in my garden, the pig-tail twist
of vines knotting and blooming
and climbing and not growing
any pumpkins at all.

I purchased the seeds in May,
drawn to the symmetry of orange
orbs on the package and the idea
of the pies, breads, and soups
I could scoop from their belly-curve.
I even loved the husked-teardrop
of their seeds, how if I held one
to light, the papery membrane
would glow like a lampshade.

Now the trees have been basted
with the yellowed glaze of fall,
and the vines sprout and finger-curl
over one another's backs. The leaves reach
dinner-plate proportions. None bear fruit.

Across the field, the sun lifts
like a swollen fruit
from the wet basket of treetops
and the bare vines stretch toward
its white-hot hallelujah.

The Weaning

A bristled cradle of hemp-cord
presses a hatched weave
into the backs of my thighs,
gritty web of chair-bottom whining
at each stiff-spined shift,
twine un-roping bit by bit
in the fringe of early light.
Birdsong coming up slow
like a half-plucked chord,
calf-bawl skimming the mist.

Yesterday a cattleman swept the pasture,
bribing heifers one by one with feed
into a lot acres over, swatting calves
with a stripped switch of birch
to stop their dogged trailing
until no pairs remained in the field.
They paced until sundown,
heifers with swollen udders trotting the fence line,
necks extended in bellows. The calves
chorused back, a ceaseless keening,
pressing forward until I was sure
the fence would buckle and the whole herd
would tumble back into one another
in a bumbling, moaning mess.

All night, wailing. Sun-up, wailing.
What unnerves me most
is that hard coil somewhere behind my ribs,
that clotted tangle of every nerve and ache
jerked still, told to hush, corralled into silence.
What unnerves me most
is how the calves won't stop screaming
and now I know
there is a wail I have kept

under my tongue for years,
and I am so afraid it might sound
just like that.

Flood Warning
>*Hath the rain a father? Or who hath begotten the drops of dew?*
>*-Job 28:38*

Dusk, and I am beckoned again
        to the slow roll and unfurl
of thunderheads in the west,
        how they hurl humid fringe
into the sunset's last wake,
        blotting dimmed violet
into dove-back gray.
        A hoarse gnarl of satisfaction
uncaged as acre after acre
        is veiled in shadow, swift
fingerlings of webbed light
        jerking in a hiss-snap squabble.

When rain claims my yard,
        the barn swallow in the house eve
fans her wings over the still-downy heads
        of her hatchlings, blue-black pinions
opaline, trembling. But I am anchored

in this downpour, each hurled drop of rain
        a horsefly sting atop my shoulders,
my sodden hair a pale whip
        gnashing my cheekbones and back.

Blind or bind me in a blistered skein
        of light, wrench me skyward
into that bitter, vexed whirl. Show me a sin
        I have not yet known, a guilt
that has never manacled my bones. There is no
        baptism in your arms. I have been here
long enough to know that none of us
        will ever be washed clean.

When It Comes Down to It

Listen: I was born to a family of evangelists and thieves,
tale-spinners and moonshiners and water-witchers,

to women with snuff bottles tucked up their sleeves,
men who knew the heft of a 'coon carcass
when the iced pelt of winter yielded nothing more.

They talked in crow-miles, in growing seasons,
in the earth's slow thaw and birth.

Their hands were chapped with the scald of lye
from scrubbing flour sack dresses down each slick rib
of a washboard. The endless plow-grip of sowing unseamed the hide
of their knuckles. They knew how to thread lies and looms,

how to unbraid the sharp of burrs from the hair
of their daughters. And yeah, they were barefoot
except on Sundays. When it comes down to it, I'm part

of the folk who've seen the blaze of God
through the tatter of corn leaves after a summer storm,
the glint of Him in the eyes of their frayed and starving kin,

they've seen Him stretch right down and bare His teeth,
and let me tell you this, they snarled right back.

Horse Thief

For my great, great grandfather, Solomon Jaggers

There was a trick to coaxing in the bit,
a massaging of the mares back gum,
his fingers working in the damp
mouth-dark just below the row
of grain-stained teeth until the gate-latch
of her jaw went slack enough to accept
the snaffle's iron bar. It was easy then,
to thread the Haflinger's ears through
the bridle's crown, to untangle her forelock
and stroke her to stillness. And then

a smoothing of the coarse hair below
her withers, easing on the saddlecloth
he would later use as a blanket.
The saddle itself he must have clutched
at his breast to keep the tack from clanging,
a sound that would surely have pulled
the blue heelers from their twitching dreams
and woken, in turn, the mare's owner.
So he stilled the buckle's fettered chatter,
tightened the girth, winced when the worn
leather chimed under his weight.

The coppered tang of night air deafened
the barn's musk as he rode from the stable,
and of course he looked back—
at the robbed barn, at the half-grown fields of tobacco
whose rows knew the even tread
of his boots, the taste of his sweat, the prayers
and curses he whispered into the black earth.

What was it that drove him to leave?
A aching that rose and settled like dust
whenever one place grew too familiar?
Or was it Kentucky, that dark and bloody ground
whose tether never let him stray too far?

And so he turned south, feeling the stolen mare's muscles
bunch and ease beneath him as they headed for a border
he knew he wouldn't reach before being caught.
Above, the balm of stars eased at his guilt, as if somehow
their long-dead light could scour him clean.

*

It had rained during the night, a here-and-gone
drizzle that beaded on the Haflinger's mane,
made her tow-pale locks slick with sweat and
rain-shed so that when Solomon reached
forward to coax her on, the strands clung
and tangled around his calloused fingers.

Near sunrise, he bedded down under a stand of pine,
removing the tack and tethering the mare,
then easing himself under a dripping canopy,
curled under the saddlecloth while dark needles
burrowed into his hair and the rough-spun
fabric of his shirt. His sleep was dreamless.

It was the mare that woke him, the quickening
of her breath near his cheek, the easy creak
her halter made as she stretched down.
And it was not surprise he felt when he saw
the horse's owner standing beside his bedroll,
a man whose fields he had plowed and planted,
a man whose table he had shared, whose daughter
he had once loved. He felt the constriction

of a noose, imagined how the rawhide would
slide past the bridge of his nose and settle
somewhere below his chin, how the rope
would sit just so between his notched vertebra
and the base of his skull.

    *

There was no trial.

Was it Solomon's words that halted the nooses
never-woven knot, that stopped some tree
from knowing the weight of his body
as it swayed from a lower limb?
What kindness made the mare's owner leave
my grandfather in some backwoods jail instead
of wringing out the justice a horse thief deserved?

Solomon never said. He told only of how he spent
a month behind a screen of rusted bars, how
in the evenings, the sun would stretch their shadows
until his cell was filled with unending columns
of dark and light. And at night, he would lie
on a mattress filled with corn husks, the
scuff of their shifting shepherding him
into dreams of home, of home, of home.

Laura May

She did not speak when they met on what passed as a road,
a muddied strip bruised with the hooves of unshod horses, boots
worn to the sole's edge, the occasional wheel-crevice of a wagon's rutting.
They traveled for silent miles in the Indiana dawn, dew-humid hair
slick on their cheekbones, stopping only when the knuckled path
caused one or the other to slip and buckle. Often, he lost sight of her
in the butterfly-winged whisk of shadows between trees, her skin
melding with the flecked bark, her feet finding the quiet space
between the stale sheddings of the forest.

*

On the second fortnight she wrapped him in a bear skin still smelling of
    wildness,
as though no matter how many times the skin had been dressed,
it still remembered the heavy muscle it belonged to, how it felt
to chuff at the den of a smaller being, to feel the yielding of ice
when a smack at a stream's edge would lend sight to the silvering bodies
of trout and catfish. When Solomon woke to her black hair spidering
across his arm, she turned and spoke, *Laura May*, a name that was hers
and not hers, and he loved her for that lie.

*

As they walked south, she sang in *Tsalagi*, coaxing a thrum from the earth
with cracked heels, her voice giving rise to some feathered thing
in Solomon's gut that wanted to startle up like a covey of quail
and beat a winged path to his throat.

*

Months passed. After the first hard freeze, the sap of the trees slid
from the ringed trunks into the webbed tangle of roots below,
and Laura fashioned a longbow from the limb of a black locust,

braiding sinew from a doe Solomon had shot with his last round
for string. She showed him how to twine the muscle from one notch to the
    other,
the ashen spindles of their breath weaving together in the branches above.

    *

They married when they reached Tell City.
The captain of a coal barge held a Bible in gloved hands
as Solomon and Laura stood on the Ohio's ice-husked edge, shivering.

    *

That night Laura May filled an abalone dish with cedar chips
and sage, pulled smoke skyward with turkey pinions as the herbs blackened
and curled, wafted offerings east, south, west, and north, to the earth, to the
    river,
and to the sky just beginning to spangle with pinpricks of flame.

She took his hands and taught him to bathe his chest and face
with the singed breath of plants. When she leaned in
and combed Solomon's hair black with bear grease,
a sheen of wildness settled into him, an embered spark that rode
on that dark current, and rose until he truly believed
that he was at last born again, and again, and again.

The Basket Trees

He preferred white oak above all else, how the grain exhaled
a sweetness that gloved his hands days after the baskets were woven.
Solomon searched for younger stands, gauged the age of each tree

by caging his palms around the trunk and squeezing as though testing
for ripeness. He harvested only the tallest saplings, knot-free and unbowed.
With a maul and wedge, he cleaved the oak's pith, the trunk splitting

like a pale quince into veined halves along vessels of wooded fiber.
From quarters to eighths to sixteenths and beyond, Solomon wrought strips
of bleached sapwood, working perpendicular to the growth rings

as his splitting knife shaved the rough sides smooth and even.
When only heartwood remained, he carried thin strips to the river's edge,
immersing them in the Ohio's ragged current until they grew pliable

as his own flesh. And then he wove, an endless over-and-under of oak rows,
a thick threading that never tangled or splintered. His grandchildren swore
his weaving was tight enough to bear water, and so let us picture him that
    way:

carrying the finished basket again to the river, filling it, then holding his
    reflection
in dripping hands. How amazed he must have been that a part of him
could be still, could be weighed, could be enough to hold and pass to
    another.

Solomon Cradles His Firstborn

A caterpillar-squirm in the crook of his arm,
swaddled body pressing and arching,
head wobbling on the flower-stem of a spine,

and then the fish-mouth caress against his breast,
the primal mother-search of tongue and gums
reaching wetly and finding only him, empty.

Surely he saw a bit of himself in that child,
an ache to be filled, mouth open, void of words,
an echo of the blank-eyed drive to end a hunger.

The Listing

Laura had begun making a list of the things Solomon stole,
beginning first with their crossing through Indiana, the scavenging
of fields he had no hand in planting, laundry unclipped
from a clothesline when the weather started to turn, and once,
a rawboned black and tan heifer they gorged on for a week
before the meat went bad. And then there was the houseboat.

Days after their marriage, he left her in the stippled dark
by the river and then called out, hours later, and told her to come aboard,
the unpracticed sweep of his rowing causing the stars to jerk
and rearrange in the black water. She hated him, then,
for her own unsteadiness, for the pale press of bone
that flared in her knuckles when she gripped the starboard rail

for balance. She hated him more as she grew to love the boat,
the nicked white paint of it's simple helm, the river's purl
against the prow, the reddened ribs of the cedar awning
they slept beneath each night, swathed in blankets
that still smelled of someone else. She began to see

Solomon's trapping as theft, too, how he lured mink
with raw crappie into travelways pocketed with iron
foothold traps and drowning locks that pulled their slick bodies
just below the surface's lip. When they docked for trade,

he always returned with a bit too much—a pound more flour
or coffee than they could have afforded, a new coat
with the wrong initials sewn into the lining,
a locket with a tintype portrait of twin boys inside, both frowning
identically at her until she peeled it from the frame
and flicked the imprinted metal into a stand of cattails.

Laura gave birth to their first daughter, Bertha, at the turn of the century.
They didn't leave the boat for weeks, spent entire days
passing the black-eyed child back and forth between them,
counting and re-counting her toes and fingers, memorizing
the crescent curve of her lips with their hands.

For a while Laura forgot the list,

but too soon Solomon was back at it, leaving each town
with a heavier rucksack and the same fistful of cash
he entered with. More children came and Laura soundlessly recited
his burglary like a lullaby as she rocked them

to sleep. On Sundays, Solomon led the children ashore
to ferret turtle eggs from the muddied sand. Bertha and her brothers
washed the taupe orbs in the water and balanced them
in damp rows in the baskets their father had woven. Laura
watched from the stern of the houseboat, placing each egg,
each new absence, on her husband's tally of theft, wondering
each time, if she should add herself to the list, too.

My Great, Great Grandfather Dreams of Returning Home

His father's empty fields: scar-tissued ruts
gone hard from neglect, dented tracks of earth
snarled with hemlock and wild onion,
a few straggles of corn beginning to tassel.

Honeysuckle clutches the house, threads
through rain-worn boards, spews
from what is left of the roof. Budded stitches
bristle in the eves, vines as thick as thumbs
holding closed a rotten wound.
The breeze holds only the candied scent
of a wild thing asking to be plucked raw
and carried home.

>   —Sadness, too, claims us in this way—
>   a quiet vineing that climbs the wet trellis
>   of our ribs and clings through each swell of breath, growing,
>   growing—

This is his homecoming.

*This is the quake in his left hand
as he jerks a vine from the crumpled doorframe.*

*This is the floorboard's molded rupture
at the weight of his step.*

*This is how it feels to fall and fall and fall
and never stop.*

Crossing out of Kentucky in a Cessna 172
For Spencer

Dusk has rinsed the land of hue: the bristle
of cornfields going a feathered charcoal,
soybean beds ashing to slate, wheat and hay
silvering into peppered granite at sundown.
Houses fleck below like a handful of cinders
rasped bright from some fire. Of course I cannot see
them, but still I imagine the stirring
of all bright-eyed night creatures, the dark flight
of bats, opossums slinking in roadside ditches,
raccoons clawing their scrawled signature
into the bark of trees. And though the engine's snarl
has deafened me from divining anything
other than the pilot's voice in my headset, I hear
the chafed chime of crickets, the quiet tap of moths
against a porch light. My Kentucky never sleeps.
Even its border, the tossing Ohio, will not be tucked in.
The river twines below us now, waxing moon
skimming it's riffled hem. Solomon had tethered his home
to that scalloped edge, his houseboat dipping and rising
with the river's wet breath. And surely
he must have seen nights like this—clear and cold
and honest and black. And surely he must have looked,
as I am, from bank to bank, above Kentucky's cedar-seeded
ridgeline and imagined a life lived differently, imagined
what it might feel like to rise from his anchoring skin, to see
the earth drop, the weight of his waking life slipping from focus,
already far from the horizon he was headed for.

Heading South

Already I am extending vowels
and dropping g's, lungs parroting

a screen door's rusted sigh, a lightning bug's click
against the pierced lid of a Mason jar.

At the state line, my heartbeat
is the dirt-shed boot stomp on a doorstep,

my blood the color of sorghum-drip,
clay-stain, cardinal wing. This is how I know

I have been away too long:
when my lover pressed his ear

to my chest, all he heard was the nine-mile echo
of a train whistle passing through

a slatted fence's wind-warped boards
and then nothing more.

Driving Through My Hometown in the Rain

I am weary of this drumming, of the spider-leg twitch
of windshield wipers, shoving aside the blur
to reveal another scab-roofed barn, another field
of cattle nosing the muddy ground.

On days like this I can almost buy it—
that we were born of earth, and climbed

from that clay womb raw-skinned,
already clawing at our salty eyes.

Homestead
> *For the Houchin family*

The mountains rose and sloped like a quilt gathered
and fanned across a lap, a calicoed drape of fir
and beech and aspen that cupped my grandfather
and his family, let them take root in the black earth,
let them cool milk in the chilled seam of stream
sewn beside their mud-chinked cabin.

Mammoth Cave bedrocked the land, held quiet the secret
of its caverns beneath, muffled the echoed slosh of fish
bleached and blind from centuries in the sandstone dark.

What path did they take, the government men who sought
my forefathers? How muddied were their boots, how briar-pocked
were their arms? Did they water their horses in that stream
when they told my family to leave? Relocation, they called it.
Federal land. A national park. A dollar per acre and a week to leave.

They carried what could be carried,
left the rest: un-ripened crops, furniture, the cabin and its floors
stained with the birth-blood of eight children.

*

The next home was bigger: two rooms,
an attic, plus front and back porches.
When the harvest was good
and enough pelts were peeled and tanned,
there were even windows with real glass.

The rough-hewn walls were plastered
with newspaper spreads: headlines of prohibition,
the invention of the radio, and the Hindenburg's
flamed descent tucked into any chink
the wind might weave through.

More children came. The house grew
smaller. The family of fifteen
sewed crops, coaxed milk
from cattle, cradled still-warm
eggs from the slatted coop out back.
At night, their feet smoothed paths
in the poplar floors on which they all slept;
knees nudged against a sister's spine, elbows
pressed against a brother's ribs, dream-talk
murmured into their mother's ear.

*

They built again:
a house of cinderblock and mortar.
No trace of sap-smell.

*

Kudzu and honeysuckle roped the old homestead. Blacksnakes
claimed the attic, knotted into muscled orbs
knit tight for warmth, their bodies finding the hollow
of a worn board where child after child had slept.
The newspapered walls yellowed and shed their layered history.
Rats chewed at the rot-soft boards and nested
in two decades worth of shredded news. The ground sighed.
The roof slumped. The windows blinked
out their panes of bevel-pooled glass.

*

The price for tobacco rose. The house with its slanting
walls and scabbed roof stood on farmland, so my grandfather
and his brothers tore down what could be used, a few shingles,
a half-dozen planks at most. It didn't take long—

there is no such thing as tedious destruction.
What remained, they burned, leaned down and lit
cigarettes from chunked embers, watched flame
trellis the porch rails, mount the stairs, lick holes
in the roof and shove it's bright, darting mouth toward the sky.

*

Before planting time, my grandfather would lead me to that field,
count off paces and walk in a square where he judged the old home
to have stood. *The kitchen was just here. And the back porch, right there.*
We walked the tilled rows and sifted the earth between our fingers,
searching for stones that would jar the setter's wheels. But always
the land birthed something new—the severed handle of a teacup,
salt cellars that were sometimes miraculously whole, and marbles,
always marbles, milked orbs veined with maple-red or shot through with
vineing green.

I kept it all, all things that the earth pushed back.
Year after year, the past rose in those rows and glinted
in the sun, aching, as all broken things do, to be made whole again.

My Great Grandmother Speaks of Wildfire

Just a rasp of cloud and light. Spark thrust down
in a haggard bolt. Twitch of wind and flame,
then a cottonmouth hiss of heat in the dark,
our barn gone bright with that timeless hunger.

Come morning, our faces were leathered with grief
or whatever lies beyond it. Smoke still guttered
from scorched beams. Whole harvest soughed off
the rafters, blistered ash piled around our ankles.

I pressed my knees into the earth, but prayer clumped
like soot in my throat. When I spat into the char,
there was only the hover of dust, hesitating, then falling.

The Last Story My Great Grandmother Told

Was of how one day she woke to a shift in the mattress, a tilting she first attributed to her husband's morning rising. But as sleep slid from her eyes, she found the bed empty, the murk of dawn already slinking west, bright splinters of sun nicking through the curtains. And again the mattress moved, flexing as though it caged some small current. Some live thing uncoiled in her stomach, too, a fear that writhed and shook the slender bones in her hand as she tossed the veiling quilt aside to reveal the vein-like rise and settle just below where her head had laid. With the dulled blade of a kitchen knife, she slit the mattress's loop-stitched seams and peeled the fabric back to expose the knotted nest of a rat snake, a stygian tangle of muscle that spiraled into itself at her intrusion. And around that black coil, hatchlings twisted in the corn husk and chicken feather bedding, narrow, obsidian bodies that slipped in and out of focus like tendrils of some black rain cloud. How long she stood watching them, she didn't know. But eventually she hauled the mattress outside, shook the bedding into the field, watched the sun-slick bodies twine away into the wheat. *Of course I didn't kill them*, she said. *After all, it was just one more mother searching to provide, to shelter her children however she could. It was just one more mother, trying.*

Passalong Plants
    For my great-grandmother, Bertha Mae Houchin

A decade after you had been committed to the ground, I treaded
past spills of daylilies, the froth of Queen Anne's Lace,
heavy stands of canna shivering like a blooded sunrise,
looking for a stand of irises.

Years ago, we watched from the stoop
as wind fish-hooked clouds all day and you spoke—
just that once—of your sister,
how there had been no word for years
until she mailed you a packet of papery bulbs
the size of garlic cloves, wrapped in rags
and packed with a note that said only:
Iris siberica, Caesar's Brother.

In truth, he never had a brother,
that orator, conqueror, marrow
of the Roman Empire—
but the iris I unearthed that day
now claims its own reign in front of my porch,
feathered sepal and amethyst overcoat.

In late fall it casts aside the scepter
of beauty, gathering the faded rinds
of petals into a pale fist.

Even now, the birch leaves rise
in husked applause.

Tornado Watch
    (Photograph of an unknown family member, 1930's)

The prow-shove of summer
pulls salt from her skin.
Knuckle-white coughs
of lightning flare
behind steaming clouds,
sky gone brassy, tense
with the wrong color.
Her hands are a blur, wings
of startled birds. Watch:
already she begins to slip
out of the frame, headed for shelter,
for some velvet-throated blossom
that will quiver at her touch.

Letters from the Arboretum

You went to seed years ago, shook a samara of fear
from your hair as you slept. I swept the floor,
swallowed it down.

    *

My hands smell of silt and ash from burying you year after year,
but the earth will not take you back. You tongue
the crumbling edges of your body and scrape the grit
from under your nails. I clear the thatch
with a rake made of rat bones and snow.

    *

Let my body be an arboretum. Lean closer:
watch fear climb the slick trellis of my ribs,
branch thickly in my throat. Watch my breath move through its limbs
like a hobbled bird with broken eyes.

    *

Your voice is a shadow so thick it slows the wind.
My pulse is a shovel, tamping down dirt.
Everything else is a lit match we pass back and forth,
licking our burned fingers until they break.

    *

Fear drips its greasy sap down my spine,
puddles in the sockets that cup my hips.
I keep the swarm of its blossoms locked
behind my teeth.
No one dares to touch me but you.

    *

You have ground your teeth against this life
until your jawbone is dust.
Tonight I will teach your name
to the blackbirds in my attic
so that they may learn to read
the tales spiders spin
in the spaces between thorns.

Drought

Nothing gave birth that summer.
The sepia-blanched corn stalks buckled
and slumped, their leaves a chafing choir
in the corkscrews of wind. The cattle grew
gaunt, lipped at what fescue the ground still bore,
huffed dust, shook flies from their eyes.
The sky was a perfect blue. Everything starved.
My grandfather told of how he daily wandered
those fields, traced the new maps the ground drew
as it split. He walked beneath the stands of poplar
and oak, their shivering canopies rusted
and fractured from thirst.

Then one morning, a crawfish hole:
a pocked steeple of clay and sod rising
above blistered ground. Inside, he saw
water—thin, rank, but filled—somehow—
with the flickered dart of minnows.

And so he dug. With his brothers, his father,
the men from neighboring farms. With shovels,
post-hole diggers, turning plows. With more doubt
than hope, they breached the silt in search of water.

Scarves of dust wreathed their shoulders,
The skin of their palms grew thin and tore,
and still they dug. No talk. Only the heavy scuff of dirt
being moved, of breath shoving past chapped lips,

and at last a sudden flex of earth, a swell and buckle
beneath my grandfather's feet—broken ground birthing
water, a wound that pooled clear and cold,
sprouted icy tendrils that crept and spread across
a grave deep hole. Then an exhale, an unwinding
of the spool-grip far below, liquid geysering
in frothed trunks and tumbles that rose and fell
and filled the pond while the men clamored
up the banks to clap and cry and fetch buckets.

When he talks of it now, my grandfather
speaks most of the Angus, how after
the men left and the pond calmed,
they gathered by the water, the latticework
of their ribs shifting as they stepped forward
and drank, how the sun set
and the moon rose on that fresh mirror,
on the rawboned cattle
anchored ankle-deep in new mud.

Buck Scouting, 1944

Daylight they hiked past frozen dung,
the iced mold of tracks, praying for a fresher sign,
a wallow, a trunk rubbed raw and shining,
bristles of hair bound in fresh sap.

Nights they roasted small game,
rabbits flushed from scrub,
squirrels with slate-gray pelts.
They licked the meat clean of ash and char,
spat bones into the fire.

And mornings, mornings were a camp of glazed graves
until each brother rose, shook off a half-foot
of snow, all of them ousting powder
from their hair, always a little awed
to break those white mounds
and stand, cold and hungry, born again.

Riverside Elegy

The river sucks scabs of bark
from the rot-soft barrels of stumps
as a shadow rises in the mud-slow waters—

a moss-veined fin, a raw mouth
searching for the needle-legged bugs
that pace near the shoreline.

I haven't fished in years,
and can barely remember how to thread
the tangled vine of a leader

or cast without snarling the line,
but still I imagine how it would feel
to pull that river-cold body onto the bank.

And of course I think of you, how instead
of tossing back my first catch, you taught me
how to fillet, guided the knife with one hand

on top of my own, patient, as though
you were pointing out constellations
in the hot, dark belly.

Riverside Elegy II

I no longer go to the river to pray.

Today I step into the stippled brim,
into the there-and-gone wake
of a bluegill's nickeled spine, balance
on the camber of bedrock, my ankles trussed in gnats.

My bones are locust legs,
all brittle grind and thrum, all kick
and shiver and scream in the heat of blood,
but I make myself still, very still.

I have no desire to be lifted
above my loneliness, no desire
to silence whatever grief it is that ricochets
from the river's root-threaded edge.

A dark wedge of geese
slips past the bluing lip of sky. At my feet,
there is only the writhe and twist
of my shadow being tugged downstream.

Coyote

> She was days dead
> and vultures had already claimed
> one tallow-soft eye, talon-worried
> her pelt into dingy clumps
> that tugged free and drifted
> like spoors in kinks of wind.
> Maggots puppeteered her hide,
> a writhing mimicry of breath
> with each swell and ebb
> in her rotting dark.
> Even the tight corpse-snarl
> was a masquerade—ants threaded
> through her graying gumline
> with the pace of the unpursued.

I was a child not yet troubled by the dead.
I hadn't learned that their names become
cinders we tuck beneath our tongues
until our throats are thick with slag.

The whine of ripe wood cast into a brushfire,
the last green tether unmoored by flame—let's pretend
our own keening is so neatly forged.
Let's greet one another by the corpses of our kin
and ignore the skate of muscle and tendon and skin
that shift in our grip as we clasp hands.
Let us not squat in the red winter wheat and tongue our
chipped teeth and place our hands upon the rot.

Let us go home.

> *Little beast, I know you now.*

Salt Lick Prayer
>*but his wife looked back from behind him, and she became a pillar of salt.*
>Genesis 19:26

Lord, often I desire to be as shameless as a cow,
particularly the unabashed manner
in which they gyrate their tongues,
lolling the slick muscle past ryegrass
and millet-stained teeth in an ardent bray
of admonishment or warning, the seemingly endless
length stretching forth in unabashed fury.

A heifer will launder the ass of a calf
in broad daylight and then return,
guiltless, the instrument of her cleaning
into her mouth. And oh! The freedom

    to explore one's own nostril with a tongue,
    to traverse the tender dark laden
    with hair and snot and grit
    with a wet appendage, and to bring that filth
    back into the most intimate realm
    of knowing, to taste the foulness
    of existence and swallow it down whole.

Dare I speak of the desire to press
my own bud-mantled tongue to all manner
of things discouraged? Once, I flattened
my mouth against the rusted pane
of a screen door until the hatched weave
bequeathed it's coppery marinade
of night wind and spider leg and wasp wing
and the salt-sweat of every palm
thrust against it. I still crave
to fasten my mouth upon every wound,
every mosquito bite, blister, and razor-slip tear.
Perhaps there is no quandary or silent ache
that cannot be solved once lapped,
but Lord, I lack the courage to bring it to my lips.

The cattle ask no absolution for flailing
their tongues, heads thrust though the perilous barrier
of barbed wire in search of crabgrass clumps,
their writhing organ a pink absurdity exposed
without even a flush in their wobbling jowls.

And see, Lord, the union of mouths at a salt lick,
not so much as a *beg your pardon*
when one greedy tongue slurps against another
in the haste to satisfy, muscled heads
nudging the weaker aside, stout shanks quaking
with the vigor of their licking, all tongues
lolling, colliding, twining, eager, naked.

Lord, let me leave this world in a cow pasture.
Omniscient, You must already know I'll take one last look
at whatever miracle or catastrophe performed
behind my back, so give me this: let it happen
when I'm surrounded by black-eyed heifers
lashing the bone-whip of their tails flank to flank
to ward off flies, udders chapped from suckling
wobble-kneed calves. Let there be discs
of excrement hard as kettle bottoms
and broom thistle necking up towards a cloudless sky.
Let there be a mockingbird on a fencepost, ranting
like the prophets must have, screeching about nothing
and everything all at once in a language
the cattle couldn't care less about.

And then, when I twist around and squint
at that forbidden thing You told me not to,
Lord, turn me into a salt lick.

Let the cows lumber forward in a heavy shuffle
of muck-chinked hooves, the frayed canopy of their lashes lit
in a sun-bright fringe. Let those tongues unfurl in crass glory
to grind wetly against my face, erasing the salted hood
of my eyelids, wearing grooves into my elbows and ribs,
eroding my fingertips and nose and that small curve of bone
at my ankles until those swaying bellies are full
of pretty much everything I was ever worth anyway.

Additional Acknowledgments

"Controlled Burn" placed third in the 2015 Green River Writers Contest for "Small Town Observations"

"Crows" placed first in the 2015 Green River Writers Contest for the category "For The Birds"

"The Weaning" placed second in the 2015 Green River Writers Contest for the category "Sometime You Can't Be Saved from Yourself"

This collection would not be possible without the love and support of my parents, Jeff and Lane Doyle, and my grandparents, Erma Houchin and the late Loy Houchin (to whom is book is dedicated), and Leroy and Loreda Vincent. My sincerest thanks goes out to the many kind and talented folks who've been involved with my education and writing life: Tom C Hunley, Mary Ellen Miller, Jonathan Travelstead, Rodney Jones, Dale Rigby, Judy Jordan, Allison Joseph, and Jon Tribble, as well as my students, past and present, who bring me continuous joy. And, of course, to my husband and best friend, Bryan.

Lesley Brower is a native Kentuckian. She earned her BA from Western Kentucky University and her MFA from Southern Illinois University Carbondale. She and her husband live in Southern Illinois, where she gardens, cooks, works for a local church, and teaches English at John A. Logan College. *Salt Lick Prayer* is her first book.

www.ingramcontent.com/pod-product-compliance
Lightning Source LLC
Chambersburg PA
CBHW070551090426
42735CB00013B/3151